(Mass.) Berlin

Memorial Record of the Soldiers of Berlin, in the Great Rebellion

(Mass.) Berlin

Memorial Record of the Soldiers of Berlin, in the Great Rebellion

ISBN/EAN: 9783337135119

Printed in Europe, USA, Canada, Australia, Japan

Cover: Foto ©ninafisch / pixelio.de

More available books at **www.hansebooks.com**

SOLDIERS OF BERLIN,

IN THE

GREAT REBELLION,

WITH THE EXERCISES AT THE DEDICATION OF THE TABLETS
OF THE DECEASED, MEMORIAL HALL, AND
THE TOWN HOUSE,

Wednesday, March 2d, 1870,

BERLIN, MASS.

———◆———

CLINTON:
PRINTED BY W. J. COULTER, COURANT OFFICE.
1870.

MUSIC.

Reading the Scriptures, and Invocation,
By Rev. W. A. Houghton.

MUSIC.

Report of Building Committee,
By Dr. E. Hartshorn.

Address accepting the Building,
By Hon. Wm. Bassett, Chairman of the Selectmen.

Dedicatory Prayer,
By Rev. Dr. Allen, of Northborough.

MUSIC.

Memorial Address,
By Rev. Mr. Houghton.

Address delivering the Tablets to the Town,
By Riley Smith of the Tablet Committee.

The Trust accepted by the Selectmen,
Through H. D. Coburn, transferring them to the care of Post 54, G. A. R.

Reply of the Post,
Through their Post Commander, E. H. Hartshorn.

MUSIC.

Poem, by Josiah Bride.

Remarks of Mr. Artemas Barnes on the early History of the Town.

Remarks by Friends, Citizens, and Non-resident Natives of the Town.

MUSIC.

Introductory Remarks.

BY DR. E. HARTSHORN.

The Hall having been well filled, Dr. Hartshorn, Chairman, at 1 1-2 o'clock called the meeting to order by a few remarks explanatory of the building, and of welcome to the non-resident natives and citizens of the town, who honored the occasion by their presence. He remarked that they were well taught in Berlin schools to read and write, and at the old town-house to vote, but were never taught there to vote till they could read and write, nor to vote anywhere with any disqualification. Remembering their experience in the old building, with its discomforts, they could imagine the pleasure which resident citizens might enjoy in their corporate capacity, surrounded by the conveniences of the new house.

Report of Building Committee.

BY DR. E. HARTSHORN, Chairman.

Mr. Chairman:

Introductory to the pecuniary part of the report of our stewardship in the construction of this building, which it is our privilege now to make to you, and through you to this assembly and the town, allow us to advert briefly to the history of the old town-house, and the discussion that gave rise to the new, as matters of interest, perhaps. to some present not acquainted with them.

The fathers of this town built their first and for the times a very liberal town hall, in the year 1831. For that purpose they appropriated a "sum not exceeding $500, above the underpinning." Timothy Bailey. Ephraim Babcock and J. D. Merriam, all of whom long since deceased. were the building committee. Abram Babcock, contractor and builder, still lives. The only furniture of the building was a stove presented by J. D. Merriam; the seats, few in number, were constituted parts of the building. That building for many years was their pride. and answered well their purposes ; but for a number of years there has been a growing desire to erect a more modern and commodious structure, and the necessity for a place of deposit for the soldiers' tablets aided to cement all opposing views in harmony.

This town has always been liberal ; were it doubted. look

at her school-houses, her military record, her tablets, her taxes so willingly borne, and now at this house, which we think not unworthy of her past history.

After discussing more expensive plans, the general outline of this building was recommended to, and adopted by the town by a full vote, and your committee were instructed to construct this building at a cost not exceeding $6,500, including the land. The idea of a decent, not to say appropriate building for such a sum was as thoroughly ridiculed, as was the capacity of the committee. We were however cheered and encouraged at the outset, by a gift of the land from an honored native and descendant of the original stock of the town, Mr. Artemas Barnes of Worcester. The town promptly returned thanks officially, and will be ever indebted for his liberality. The spot we deemed eminently suitable, and posterity will approve it. The owners of the old horse-sheds, which marred the beauty of our common and nearly destroyed the value of this land, should be commended for their readiness to yield at once for their removal. Thanks are also due to the religious society for allowing free use of their grounds, for the same purpose. The sheds were removed and fitted up at considerable expense, it is true, but no witty criticisms upon their removal or upon the spot will abide the test of time. If nothing had been gained but the removal of this unseemly blemish, the expense would be well repaid.

The principles upon which this particular plan of economy and style were adopted, were briefly these, viz : The old house accommodated the town, with a regular growth, more or less perfectly, for thirty-nine years, and the plan adopted in this building may convene the same proportionate growth as long. But if by fortunate enlargement of business its growth should be more rapid, then it will have the wealth of that growth to expend anew. Again, a build-

ing like this is more appropriate in comparison with our
humble style of buildings, and for many years may remain
so. Still again; the style of architecture and the taste of
the citizens might change with time, increasing business
and wealth. Our old house was as consonant with the
taste, style, necessities, desires, and conveniences even, of
our fathers, as this will be with ours. Thirty years some-
times work great and unanticipated changes in a thrifty
town. We hope for great things, but have not the positive
assurance of them. Once more, a small audience in a hall
like this, (and comparatively small will be the audiences
here for some years at least)—we say a small audience will
enjoy more, and be more inviting to a speaker, than the
same audience in a hall large enough for the crowd that
may flock here weekly thirty years hence. The pleasure
during these years of an audience-room proportioned some-
what to the size of the audience, will compensate the
expense of a new house at the end of that time, if necessary. Upon the basis of these principles we built ; upon
the same reasoning we invite your criticism of the size, the
style, the plan, the convenience, the fixtures, the furniture,
the arrangements in general, hoping you may, charitably at
least, approve our work.

For the Building Committee allow me to say, personally,
that perfect harmony and entire oneness of feeling has been
manifested in all their deliberations, and they have the
thanks, at least, of their chairman.

To you, sir, and the board of Selectmen individually, we
return thanks for very numerous cheering words of support,
encouragement and co-operation, and also to the citizens
generally who have shown their confidence in us, and our
work, by approving remarks.

Especially are our thanks due to the contractors, Messrs.
S. H. Hastings, J. E. Sawyer and Addison Keyes, who have

completed this work to our entire satisfaction. During the
entire progress of the building we have not had occasion to
find the least fault with any point of their work. We com-
mend them as men of skill, who from thoroughly con-
demned material a beautiful structure can raise.

In conclusion, Mr. Chairman, we cheerfully give this
house to your care. We are not ashamed of it, nor would
we essentially alter it if we could. We undertook its erection with fears, but our doubts have been crowned with success beyond our hopes. Hand it over to the town with our
best wishes. We shall soon pass away. A few for a very
few years will remember that many weary hours were spent
in planning and arranging this structure, then none will be
left who will care who did it. Year after year the people
will come up here to transact important business for the
town, the state, and the nation ; our hope is that they may
do it in all good conscience. Here they will listen to men
of eloquence in science and morals, and may they give heed
to their instructions. Should false doctrines ever be taught
here, may they fall as if on stony ground, where they will
take no root. May prosperity fill this house, so that long
before another thirty-nine years elapse, the growth of the
town may compel the erection of a larger, nobler structure.
May the coming generations remember that they are some-
what indebted to their fathers, and especially may they re-
vere their fathers' God, and we will be content with our
mission as we are crowded off the stage.

Allow us to report with pleasure, that the entire cost of
this building (including another coat of paint and blinds
painted and hung) above the underpinning is $6.000. The
cost of removal of sheds and their repair, the fitting of the
ground, and the foundations so far as completed, is $446.64
—making in all $6,446.64, as the entire cost of the proper-
ty. The cost of furniture at the time the town voted to

Address Accepting the Building.

BY HON. WM. BASSETT.

Mr. Chairman:

Sir,—It is ever cause of gratulation when those engaged in the public service, in the discharge of their duties have faithfully executed the trust confided to them, and whose chief aim has been, with an eye single to the public good, fully to carry out the will of the people. Permit me then to extend to you an assurance of the high satisfaction which the people of this town (so far as I may represent them) have of the manner in which you and those associated with you on the committee, have planned and finished this house so well fitted for the convenience of the town. We are aware that you have had some difficulties to encounter—some obstacles to overcome ; but your energy and perseverance have been equal to the occasion, and to-day the verity of the estimates presented have been completely sustained, and the tax-payers of the town have been agreeably surprised to find that their committee have been enabled to bring the cost of the building within the sum asked for. At the beginning there was a diversity of opinion as to the general plan and details, but as the work progressed more unanimity of feeling was expressed, and now scarcely a dissenting voice is heard. The building in its exterior is humble and unpretending, and in general accord with the surrounding buildings in the town ; but in its interior it is believed to combine the greatest amount of convenience at the least possible expense, and is well calculated to supply the present and prospective wants of the town.

The town was greatly in need of the conveniences furnished by this house, for social and municipal purposes, and also on festive and public occasions ; and it was but in accordance with the progressive spirit of the age, this resolution of the town, to give to themselves, to the officers of the town and to the soldiers returned from the late war, a suitable place for meeting and consultation ; but not least was it the intention that a more fit place should be prepared for the reception of the soldiers' memorial tablets, which are to transmit to future generations the names of those who perished in the great rebellion, fighting for the preservation of our liberties, that we might have a "government of the people, for the people and by the people ;" and in conclusion permit me to say that the ability and fidelity by you manifested in the erection of this house, is duly appreciated by those who in the beginning reposed full confidence that their committee chosen for the purpose was equal to the task imposed on them.

build was estimated at $1,000. Much better furniture and
fixtures than were then contemplated have been procured
at an expense of $952.00, making the entire cost of build-
ing and furniture $7,398,64.

Should the next town-house cost as much more than this
as this has cost more than the old one, the amount will be
$100,000, a sum which perhaps then will not be satisfac-
tory to the sticklers for a costly town house.

To you and your coadjutors we again return thanks for
your kind aid in this enterprise, as we hand you the keys of
this structure ; may they always fall into as worthy hands.

E. HARTSHORN,
RILEY SMITH,   *Building*
SILAS SAWYER,
GEO. H. BARNES,   *Committee.*
DANIEL CARTWRIGHT,

MEMORIAL ADDRESS.

BY REV. W. A. HOUGHTON.

FELLOW-CITIZENS OF BERLIN:

We do not expect that the 2d of March, 1870, will henceforth be especially memorable in Berlin for the dedication of a town-house. Once we dedicated churches only. Once there were no town-houses to dedicate. Churches, very generally, served the purposes of town meetings, and these were about the only meetings aside from the Sabbath.

I take it that Faneuil Hall is the oldest town-house in America, and that not quite a hundred and thirty years old. It would have been older, but the town of Boston, like some other ambitious boroughs, refused to accept it of the generous Peter on the conditions he made. The proposed "market" under it was the objection. Boston did not believe in any such "notion." No town-house in our vicinity is over fifty years old. Our old one is less than forty. We honor our fathers for such a house as that ; but our needs are much greater than in 1831. Not so much because our population has doubled as because our ideas have. Berlin is of the progressive towns. And to anticipate the more ambitious Berlineans who shall take this house down or sell it, as we do the old, we will here say, we hardly expect this comely edifice to satisfy the town in 1900. Our judicious committee put no memorials under the corner stone, lest the lads who should have seen them put in would also see them taken out. But we are willing to be judged, even in the twentieth century, by our present work.

Religious dedication of public buildings is very suitable. Some may think it is secularizing religion. We think it is making secular matters properly religious. The public edifice, the private dwelling, the house of business, that cannot be religiously dedicated, ought not to be built.

All our present public buildings have been built by the town—the church, the school-houses, this house and its predecessor. About one in ten of us remember the first "meeting-house." A few are living who were in childhood when it was raised. A huge pile of architecture it seemed to some of our eyes when we first saw it in its decline. Its remains compose the frame-work of our neighbor Fosgate's barn. Sad end for the old sanctuary; but honorable. Martyred soldiers' bones have been used for fertilizers.

The church which adorns the common and the village was built when the town was one parish, forty-four years ago.

Public buildings are an index of the taste and spirit of a town. We are willing our fathers should be judged by the criterion, as we expect to be.

Twelve years ago the town erected new school-houses in the five districts, at a cost of nearly seven thousand dollars; just in time before the war. They have justly been a source of pride and of praise.

The question of a new town-house began to be agitated before the war, but lay quiet, mostly, during that great burden and sorrow. Except for railway and new roads the question would have revived sooner. But the deciding point lay in the adoption of tablets and memorial hall for our dead soldiers, instead of a monument. No monument could be raised, satisfactory to the citizens, short of three

thousand dollars. Some preferred hall and tablets. The
point was conceded. and the question of town-house was
decided.

The constructing committee make their report to-day, and
I am sure the opinion which I express is not individual, but
common. We owe a special debt of grateful recognition to
this committee and the faithful executors of their specifica-
tions, the builders ; and I know I but speak for the public
when I make special mention of the chairman. The plan
is essentially his. In style of finish he has had the co-operation of his colleagues and the builders, embracing professional good judgment. Only by the most judicious pur-
chases and strictest watch and supervision could the house
have been built for the sum reported. In all this, too, the
judicious and honorable principle has been adopted to expend, so far as economically practicable, the town money
within the town, a thing (to moralize a little) this town has
painful need of learning. Why send your money out of
town needlessly, for professional skill or the commodities of
life, when you can have the same at home? Every town
ought to have its *esprit de corps.* Whoever refuses his pat-
ronage to a good citizen, works against his own and the
town's welfare. This house is a home production.

A town-house and a town-hall are not precisely the same.
Peter Faneuil did not count on "selectmen's room" and
other such apartments, but on a meat market. We are not
so sensual. Lyceums, literary associations, reading rooms,
public libraries belong to these edifices. It is to be hoped
that all these may yet pertain to our own. Let this house
be consecrated to all liberal improvement and culture ; and
it is a hope of many that it may never be desecrated by
uses injurious to the public. What depraves the morals of
a people, in the youth, or others, is unprofitable every way.
Mountebanks and jim crow dances do the least of their

mischief when they carry out of town and out of the pockets of our youth in a single night money to the amount of any young man's yearly savings. Better let your house stand close as the temple of Janus in peace. Such income will never equal what is carried out of town, even in money. The "town fathers" should not make a losing bargain for their town family. You get ten dollars for the town, and the town is fifty dollars poorer, by count of dollars. When our own citizens use it, and take money one of another, that is interchange. Or a concert, a lecture, by strangers, may leave in worth of intellectual wealth, more in value than they carry away in money. But the fathers of the town should be as judicious in all such interchange of value for value, as the father of a family.

Let this hall never be ruled by any illiberality of sentiment. Let it be a place of all generous culture—a place of genial, social and refining enjoyments ; but not a means of public demoralization.

We dedicate this principal hall to town interests and uses, first of all. Few will be the assemblies here of so much importance as the "Town Meeting." In this hall annually, and repeatedly, the town will come together in that democratic capacity which, more perfectly than any other, represents the common spirit of American institutions. De Toqueville, that comprehending Frenchman, was profoundly impressed with the relation of the towns in America to the commonwealth. The reality had been illustrated in the action of towns in the Revolutionary struggle. It has been more forcibly illustrated of late. But our hope is that this hall may never resound with the war cry as we have heard it heretofore. If need be, let that be heard. But our hope is, and our prayer, that national peace may leave every town to the development of their own interests and the enjoyment of their own social privileges.

The town meeting is an educator. Citizens, in this, enter jointly into consideration of the questions which mostly concern the public welfare. Narrow ideas are here liberalized. Extravagant ideas are sobered. Steel encounters steel. The result is, generally, practical good sense. If anywhere men are "weighed," it is in the town meeting. The true wisdom of a poor man will outweigh the folly of any exalted position ; and every man's vote counts the same. The theory of such pure democracy is that every voter is a "true man," and will seek only what he regards as the public good, and the vote is too sacred a trust to be used for personal or mere party ends. He whose eye is not on the public good in voting, is not worthy of the ballot. He ought to live where he can be ruled.

The town meeting is not a debating society, and no unnecessary antagonisms should ever be made. But the necessary issues of all public questions call out the best powers of expression in any citizen who has thoughts to offer. Your speaker recalls town meetings of more than forty years ago, in the old meeting-house. I have ever since been more interested in town meetings than in any mere debating societies. I am instructed by them to this day. I thought, forty years ago, that the fathers were great men. I appreciate them equally now. But the matters and business of this town today far exceed the responsibilities of the fathers, yet these interests do not suffer in present hands ; and after some observations abroad, I am glad to say of my native town, and of my own fellow-citizens, that I think we fall behind very few towns in the number, relatively, or in the ability of citizens, who can appropriately express themselves, and ably discuss such questions as pertain to the public concerns. I have noticed, with pleasure, that we have a large number of citizens of apt ability to preside in our public assemblies with appropriateness and efficiency.

May the new facilities which this house offers us for various social, literary, or other public assemblages, become a new stimulus to our youth and young men to improve their various talents in such ways as shall be creditable alike to themselves and to the public character of the town. It is but reasonable that this commodious and attractive public edifice should become a new bond of unity in the town.

Fellow-citizens, this town is compact in territory; very few families live two miles from this spot. We have several clusters of dwellings ; but none for whose interest it is to be separated, even socially, from the others. If we of the centre are more benefitted than others by this public improvement, it is not of a selfish gratification to us. The centre, I know, would that all could be equally benefitted. Our territory is so compact, and the centre so easily accessible to every village at least, that some of us have looked forward in hope of a consolidation of our school districts into graded schools.

The town has two railway stations, and hopes for a third better than both these. Business interests are making hopeful headway. It should be the object and effort of every citizen to promote it. Home interests should be the mutual effort of all citizens. We have no villages that desire annexation to a more pretentious neighbor. None that desire to set up for themselves in township. Any family, in a few years residence, may know every other family connected with the town. For ten years past almost every winter examination of schools in each district has been attended by spectators from every other district in the town. The success and character of each school is a town interest, and I believe that every village is really interested in the prosperity of each. May no strife worse than a lawful emulation ever exist.

Citizens, personally, I rejoice in the eighteen years' re-

newed citizenship in my native town. I have a home with
you ; I have a burying place with you. But a minister's
calling is such as forbids him to give "commandment con
cneringhis bones." I have read eloquent sermons introductory to a minister's "first love," expressing ardent desire that
the preacher might be buried among his "dear people." I
have met these "fellow servants" years after, well clothed,
as to their "bones," far from their dear people, as to local-
ity, and farther still in heart.

But I must say the thought is pleasant of being buried
in my native town with my fellow-citizens ; yet my greater
anxiety is to join with you all, while my citizenship contin-
ues, in earnest co-operation in whatever shall be for the
town's true interests.

Will you allow me, citizens, to say, representatively, that
the day of *religious* acrimony is gone by. I hope you all
hold your religious faith in a good conscience. But sure I
am that difference of belief is no occasion of social animos-
ities. It seems to me that a hopeful day is opening upon
Berlin, as to social life and general prosperity ; and let us
accept the kind providence of the God of our fathers in
the erection of this beautiful and commodious house, as a
pledge of His good will to us as a people, and as a bond of
renewed union as a town. We extend greeting to those
once of us, and with us for today. We send greeting to
all such who are abroad. We are often cheered in reports
of their worth to other communities. We greet our neighboring towns also, and rejoice with them in their prosperity.

This house has another and peculiar bond of unity to
this town : the *Memorial Hall*, commemorative of our honored soldiers, deceased. This was the pivot on which
turned the question of erecting this house at the present
time.

How far from our thoughts it was, in 1860, that in 1870

we should consecrate our proposed new edifice to the memory of a score of our young men and fellow-citizens, in honor of laying down their lives for us in the conflicts of war. What years of history the last decade! The opening act of war was read to a body of citizens at the post-office before the coach bringing the mail of April 12th, 1861, had left the door. Few were the words spoken. But every man set his lips in defiance. The war fever took, at the flash, in Berlin. War meetings followed in quick succession. Young men did not falter. The zeal was no fanaticism. In tears many resolved on the forbidding service. Scores were soon pledged. Had the way been clear, a full company of a hundred would have been organized in this population of a thousand. Of course no man could apprehend the coming realities, but the pledges were soberly made. Delays cooled off impetuous ardor. But if less manifest, the tide of patriotism flowed in deeper channels. The impulse of patriotism that rolled over the land became like the still small voice after the thunder. There was no holy of holies in the household nor sanctuary which it did not enter. Thought of the strange work to which they were called would have chilled the blood before the call came. Now it hurries up the life current, and gives nerve to manhood strength. The beauty of Israel was ready for the offering. Berlin was never behind in response, during the war—often in advance. We had, in all, in the terrible service, one hundred and thirty-nine men. Of these, twenty-two offered up their lives on the field or in army service.

We are gathered today in special commemoration of their unselfish and patriotic valor. We meet to embalm their names. This house we expect will perish. The chaste marble that speaks now may be destroyed. But we pledge ourselves in sacred honor and grateful obligation never to

3

forget, but ever to cherish the names and character of those who faced death and fell in his embrace for our liberty. Their portraits which grace the same hall may fade from the material on which they are impressed in such life-like features, but coming years will only add to the honor in which they are now held.

That we may more fully enter into this specialty of the hour, let me, in briefest manner, remind you of the

THE PERSONAL HISTORY OF THE FALLEN.

And let me say here, that the obtaining and the verification of the necessary particulars is very difficult. Our official returns have not been made in full. Such as were made are frequently incorrect, according to the testimony of soldiers.

Captain " C. S. Hastings," a name for years as familiar in Berlin as the name of the town, properly heads the death roll of our deceased soldiers. Christopher Sawyer Hastings, son of Ephraim and Achsah Hastings, was born in Lancaster, now Clinton, in 1814. Moses was the name by which he was called till he became of age, when he changed it to Christopher. His childhood and youth were spent in Boylston, whither his parents removed. At twenty-one years he came to Berlin, his father having purchased the Nathan Johnson estate. In 1840 he settled himself in the family state with Miss Cordelia Bigelow of Marlboro', on the homestead which he so much adorned in various improvements. He was a citizen in the true sense, active and enterprising—a man of cheerful social habits, and public spirited as a townsman. His fellow-citizens bestowed upon him important trusts, which he ever met with fidelity. At the opening of the war his age exempted him from military service. His offering was voluntary. True, he had much at stake, with others. But he had no doubt of the final issue. yet he would not withhold his own personal service. He enlisted in Co. I. 36th Regt. Mass. Vols., and entered into the service as captain. September, 1862. The regiment was about Harper's Ferry awhile. and the upper Potomac ; then at Fredericksburg, and under fire in that battle. but not engaged. Their next service was in the southwestern department. Capt. Hastings was with his regiment in the seige of Vicksburg. and three days in the engagement at Jackson. Here he sickened, and was left behind the regiment, on its return to Kentucky. He recovered and wrote his last letter at Memphis. returning to his regiment. Was taken sick again, and died at Mound City, Ill.. Sept. 8th. 1863. at 49 years of age.

Thomas Rathburn. son of Solomon H. and Hannah Rathburn. was born in Bolton. 1841. Rathburn made the first regular enlistment of our soldiers. though he did not go on that enlistment. July 4th. 1861. he was enrolled in Co. F, 13th Regt. Mass. Vols. The early service of the regiment was tedious in marches. On the upper Potomac, on picket duty. he contracted a fever of which he died at Winchester. March 14th, 1862, at 20 years of age. His remains. the first of our death harvest in the war, were sent home in charge of his fellow soldier. Corporal S. H. Haynes, and were buried in our own cemetery.

Charles H. Maynard. son of Charles H. and Priscilla Maynard (Mrs. Reuben Babcock), was born in Stow, April 11th, 1835. Resident here at the outbreak of the war. he was among the first to enlist for our defense. He joined Co. E, 13th Regt. Mass. Vols., in July, 1861. He zealously followed the fortunes of this brave regiment in all its perils and hard service of movements and battles, till the memorable day of Gettysburg, when he was taken prisoner. Exchanged. he declined in health. and died in service of the invalid corps, at Douglas Hospital. Washington, D. C., Jan.

24th, 1864, at 28 years of age. His grave is in our own cemetery.

Alonzo F. Howe, son of Lyman and Rebecca Howe, was born in Marlborough, March 24th, 1831. Just before the war he raised here his domestic sanctuary, and gathered his little family around him. He enlisted in Co. H, 29th Regt. Mass. Vols., Dec. 23d, 1861. He was unable, much of the time, to do field duty, but was with his regiment at the seige of Vicksburg. Returning, he was taken sick on the way, and died at Camp Denison, Cincinnati, Sept. 7th, 1863, aged 32 years. His remains were brought to this place for burial.

Silas F. Jillson (misnamed Gilsom on tablet), son of Wheaton C. and Eliza B. Jillson, was born in Richmond, N. H., May 24th, 1863. Living in this town at the opening of the war, he readily enlisted for the town in Co. I, 25th Regt. Mass. Vols., Oct. 20th, 1861. Jillson was the first of our soldiers to receive a wound. This at Roanoke Island. He continued in the service through the war, but died at Charlotte, N. C., July 14th, 1865, aged 29 years. He received a second wound in the Summer of 1864.

Silas E. Goddard, son of Ephraim and Sophia Goddard, was born in Berlin, March 24th, 1832. A retiring, modest youth, a dutiful son, of infirm health, he nevertheless was urgent to go at the call of his country ; and enlisted in Co. I, 36th Regt. Mass. Vols. Was in the Vicksburg campaign, but sunk in sickness on return to Kentucky, and died at Camp Nelson, Sept. 10th, 1863, at 21 years of age. His letters were full of courage, though comrades affirm that he was often really unable to do duty.

George Ira Carter, son of Ira and Hannah Carter, was born in Berlin. He enlisted Aug. 6th, 1862, in Co. I, 36th Regt. Mass. Vols. Among the youngest of all our soldier boys, he followed closely the service of his regiment, and

was in all its engagements. Was wounded at Poplar
Spring Church, Va., being shot through the left lung ; was
taken prisoner, and died at Petersburg, Sept. 30th, 1864,
20 years old. It is related of him that in battle, the regiment being under fire, he refused to lie down at orders, but
stood till the word of "charge" was given, when he tossed
his gun in air and caught it as he plunged with the rest
into the deadly strife.

Hollis L. Johnson, son of Lewis H. and Mary Johnson,
was born in Berlin, June 7th, 1838. Spent most. of his
youth among us. Enlisted in Co. F, 13th Regt. Mass. Vols.,
1862. He was in constant service till his death, which oc-
curred at the second battle of Bull Run, Aug. 30th, 1864.
A long and painful suspense hung over his parents and
friends as to his lot in that battle. Up to this point he had
kept up frequent correspondence with the family at home.

Thomas Hastings, son of Reuben and Hannah Hastings,
born in Berlin, Jan. 24th, 1818. Married Elizabeth T.
Houghton of Bolton, in which town he resided some years.
Enlisted in Co. C, 15th Regt. Mass. Vols. He went through
the Peninsula campaign, and was at the battle of Antie-
tam, from which only fifteen of the company came out. A
ball passing through both his legs above the knee, he was
left upon the field. He succeeded in reaching an old barn,
with others, where they remained four days, helping each
other as they could, when they were removed to Campbell
Hospital, Philadelphia. Chronic diarrhœa having set in,
he died Oct. 23d, 1862, at 44 years of age.

Nathan B. Garfield was born in Shrewsbury. His youth
was spent partly in Amherst, N. H. He came to this place
from Marlboro', a diffident and retiring young man, the last
of all, we should have said, to make a soldier. But none
were more ready at duty's call for any conflict. Repeatedly rejected for bodily frailty, his spirit burned to serve his

country. Was finally accepted in Co. 1, 25th Regt. Mass.
Vols., July, 1862. Garfield served his regiment mainly in
the hospital. Yet nothing but the field would satisfy his
zeal. The field he took, and on the field he fell at Bermu-
da Hundred, Va., May 16th, 1864. aged 29 years. He
was tenderly buried by his fellow soldier, Eli Sawyer, Jr.,
of this town.

William H. Coburn, son of Henry D. and Hannah Coburn, was born in Berlin, 1841. Very thoughtfully, and
with parental consent, he. enlisted in Co. I, 36th Mass.
Vols., Aug. 6th, 1862. From the battle of Fredericksburg
he accompanied the regiment to the seige of Vicksburg ;
was taken sick after the battle of Jackson, and was brought
to Portsmouth Grove Hospital, R. I. Was again on duty
in the battle of the Wilderness. in which he was wounded
in a charge on the enemy's works, May 6th, 1864. The
wound was in the thigh. After many removals, with great
suffering, he was brought to Campbell Hospital, Washington, where he died Sept. 18th, 1862, aged 21 years. He
had the great consolation of his brother's attendance in his
last days. I cannot forbear to give one extract of a letter
dated May 16th. 1864 : "Dear Sister, I feel happy that I
can write you. I am lying on my back in an Episcopal
church here in Fredericksburg. with a little book in my left
hand, while I write with the other. My wound pains me
some, and the bed is not as good as you have at home. I
have one blanket and two pieces of tent spread on the hard
floor. As I lie here I can look out and see the trees all
leaved out, and here the birds sing. But I am a caged bird
now, and so must stay in one place. I think half the men
here that live would have died but for the Christian Commission."

James H. Barry was born in Nova Scotia. 1844. Spent
his youth under the fatherly care of Henry D. Coburn of

this town. He eagerly enlisted in Co. I. 36th Mass. Vols., July, 1862. Barry was in the battles of the regiment at Fredericksburg. Vicksburg. Jackson. Knoxville, the Wilderness, Spottsylvania. North Anna. Cold Harbor, and was instantly killed on picket duty, in front of Petersburg, July 1st, 1864, the ball passing through his right arm and body. He exclaimed, "My God, my God!" and ceased to breathe. His fellow soldier, Ansel Snow, assisted in his proper burial beside the Norfolk and Petersburg Railroad. Aged 20 years.

Samuel A. Snow, adopted son of Ansel Snow of Berlin, was born in Milford. son of Samuel A. and Susan Salsbury, 1845. Enlisted in Co. I. 25th Regt. Mass. Vols., Oct. 14th, 1861, and followed closely the service of his regiment. Was in battle at Romanoke Island. Newbern. Kingston, Whitehall, Goldsboro', Port Walthall, Arrowfield Church, N. C. Re-enlisted, as veteran, when the regiment came to Virginia, and was taken prisoner at Drury's Bluff. May 27th, 1864. He endured the cruelties of Libby and Andersonville until October, when he was taken to Savannah, thence to Florence, S. C., where he died Dec. 1st, at the age of 19. Such was the soldier life of a timid, retiring boy, hardly known among us, only as a pupil in our schools.

George H. Bowers was born in Boston. Came to this town a stranger, with his family, two years before the war. Enlisted in Co. I, 36th Regt. Mass. Vols., September, 1862. Died of disease at Covington. Ky., Sept. 30th, 1863, aged 36 years. Particulars of his death unknown.

Edwin J. Bigelow, son of Horace and Almina Bigelow, early enlisted in service of his country, but was discharged on account of ill health. Re-enlisted 1864, in 61st Regt. Mass. Vols., and was killed in making a charge on the enemy's works in front of Petersburg. Va., April 2d, 1865, aged 20 years.

Rufus H. Williams, son of Rufus and Sarah Williams, born in Bolton, 1843, was not liable to military duty, but was urgent to go, and enlisted in Co. I, 25th Regt. Mass.. Vols., 1861. Died of disease at Georgetown, D. C., April 4th, 1862, at the age of 19 years.

Henry P. Rich, son of James and Sally Rich, was born in Northborough, 1845. Enlisted 1864, in Co. D, 4th Battalion Heavy Artillery, at Fort Independence, where he died of disease Aug. 11th, 1865, at the age of 20 years.

Tyler Paine, born in Smithfield, R. I., had been a citizen of Berlin some years. At enlistment he had four motherless children. He neverthless gave himself to his country in her need. Enlisted in Co. B, 2d Mass. Cavalry. The regiment was in the Red River expedition, from which, on return to New Orleans, Mr. Paine died of disease, June 15th, 1864, aged 40 years. Enlisted Jan. 5th, 1864.

Homer E. Stone, son of Isaac and Martha Stone, was born in Berlin, June 24th, 1843. The health of his parents kept him awhile from enlistment. He finally joined the 4th Regt. Mass. Cavalry, Co. E, September, 1863. His frequent letters are full of patriotism and affection. "I know," he says, "the cause I am in is right, as sure as there is a God." "I am reconciled to my lot." He remitted many drawings of his own, representing forts and scenery about the James. His service was short. In June, 1864, he contracted disease of which he died July 24th, near Petersburg, aged 21 years.

Lafayette Warden was born in Illinois. Name of parents unascertained. His home among us was principally with Mr. Harvey D. Carter. Was mustered into service in Co. C, 15th Regt. Mass. Vols. Died of wounds at Washington, D. C., June 15th, 1864, aged 22 years. He attained to the rank of first duty Sergeant.

Watson Wilson, son of James and Persis Wilson. En-

listed in Co. I, 36th Regt. Mass. Vols., Aug. 27th, 1862.
Died of wounds received at Cold Harbor, June 3d, 1864.

Charles D. Starkey, son of Anthony S. and Martha Starkey, was born in Berlin, July 18th, 1838. He spent his youth among us. His health was not firm, but he enlisted, 1862, in Co. I, 5th Regt. Mass. Vols., for nine months' service. He was in the several engagements of his regiment in North Carolina, but sickened and died at Newbern, May 26th, 1863, aged 25 years. His comrades testify to his vol untary over exertions, by which sickness was induced.

Lemuel Gott, Jr., son of Dr. Lemuel and Mary Gott, born in Rockport, Cape Ann, Feb. 20th, 1840, came to this town with his father's family in 1855. He graduated at the Normal School, Westfield, in 1862 ; afterwards was Principal of High School in Danville, Ill. In the midst of great usefulness, sickness compelled him to resign. Recovering, he was eager for the field. As a trial of strength, he enlisted in Co. I, 5th Regt. Mass. Vols., for one hundred days' service. Suffering a sunstroke his health failed, fever set in and he died in hospital at Baltimore, Aug. 29th, 1864, attended by his father. His grave is with us. He was 24 years of age, an only son and brother, of great promise to friends and society.

DIED AFTER DISCHARGE FROM THE ARMY.

J. P. N. Johnson, more familiarly known as Pillsbury Johnson, son of Edward and Annie Johnson, was born in Berlin, 1824. He enlisted in Co. F, 15th Regt. Mass. Vols., and was in much of its service till the winter of 1862-3. After some service at Columbia Hospital, Gorgetown, D. C., he was discharged from the army, Feb. 3d, 1863, on account of ill health. Returning home he declined gradually, and died May 20th, 1864, aged 40 years.

William Florence, son of Daniel G. and Mary Florence,

born in Marlboro', enlisted in Co. I, 36th Regt. Mass. Vols., 1862. Was honorably discharged for ill health in February, 1863, at Newport News He gradually declined and died in Berlin May 5th, 1863, aged 23 years.

Ezra Bartlett, son of William and Sarah Bartlett, born in Berlin, enlisted for the one hundred days' service in the Summer of 1864. At Indianapolis, Ind., on guard of rebel prisoners, he contracted fever, of which he died at Camp Carrington, Oct. 16th, aged 19 years.

George E. Hartwell enlisted September. 1862, in Co. F, 13th Regt. Mass. Vols. Was discharged by surgeon's certificate, and died in Hudson, Feb. 15th, 1863. The Hudson Encampment have erected a tablet over his grave.

Mr. Riley Smith, in behalf of the Tablet Committee, remarked as he gave the tablets in charge of the town:

Gentlemen, Selectmen of Berlin:

You are well aware that two years ago a committee was appointed to procure four tablets for those soldiers and heroes of Berlin who dared to die in defence of their flag, and to sustain their country. That committee was composed of Rev. Wm. A. Houghton, Hon. Wm. Bassett, Israel Sawyer, A. W. Longley and myself. The committee has attended to that part of their duty. and have procured four tablets, and placed them upon the walls of Memorial Hall below. After visiting different artists and viewing different specimens of materials and workmanship, we contracted with B. H. Kinney of Worcester, this State, for the same, whose artistic skill and workmanship is excelled by no one in the State. We had the uttermost confidence in his honor as a man and his skill as an artist.

We contracted with him for four tablets at $125.00 apiece, making in all $500.00, as voted by the town.

I have been delegated by that committee to present those beautiful tablets to you, gentlemen, and intrust them to your care. They wish you to accept them, not for their intrinsic value alone, but in deep commemoration of those heroes whose names are chiseled on those tablets. And, if you please, accept them in great reverence to those heroic soldiers on my left, *their* comrades and associates in the din of battle and deadly strife for victory.

Please to accept in great respect to those fathers and mothers, brothers and sisters, widows and orphans of those martyred heroes, who feel that they have sacrificed their dearest idol upon the altar of liberty, and for the benefit of their country and its union. Their hearts bleed and their homes are made vacant by this sad event.

And finally, accept them and make such disposition of them as shall be pleasing to yourselves, the soldiers present, and to the citizens of the town.

ACCEPTANCE OF THE TABLETS, BY MR. H. D. COBURN, OF THE SELECTMEN.

GENTLEMEN OF THE COMMITTEE:

In behalf of the inhabitants of the town of Berlin, we accept these beautiful tablets, so commemorative of our deceased soldiers. We most sincerely thank you for your faithful and successful services in planning, procuring, and arranging them in our Memorial Hall. Forever may they perpetuate the memory of those who nobly gave their lives a sacrifice on their country's altar to secure for us the blessings of peace and the enjoyment of our pleasant and happy homes.

To you, sir, Commander of Post 54 of the Grand Army of the Republic, we give these Memorial Tablets in charge,

to be sacredly guarded by you and those in your command
against all ruthless and rude hands, that they may never be
injured or marred, but remain in our Memorial Hall to perpetuate the memory of our deceased soldiers. It is to be
distinctly understood that they are to be open to the visita-
tion of the soldiers and the inhabitants of the town, their
families and friends, at any and all reasonable times, in
charge of careful and competent attendants. May they
ever remain to show to future generations our patriotism
and the love and respect we have for our deceased soldiers.

REPLY OF POST COMMANDER E. H. HARTSHORN.

Acting as Commander of this Grand Army Encampment
—though unworthy of the honor, either by active service or
personal sacrifice—I am called upon to represent those who
have fought my battles as well as yours.

In accepting the charge of these beautiful tablets erected
by you in memory of our departed comrades, we assure you
that to no better hands could you entrust them, for they
have faced suffering and death side by side with those who
have fallen, and will appreciate as you cannot their sacrifice. The soldiers need no tablets to remind them of those
they miss in their scattered ranks, for their memories and
deeds of valor are written deep in their hearts—written
while midst the noise of battle they cheered each other to
renewed zeal, or stayed for a moment the onward charge
to support a dying comrade and receive the last messages of
love for dear ones at home. Memories such as these death
alone will end ; memories that, though constant, find expression each year as they strew their graves with flowers.

We accept this trust for ourselves. We accept it in behalf of those whose dear ones left them never to return,
save in death's cold embrace, and who, with wounded hearts

opened afresh by the recital of their daring deeds and self-sacrificing spirit, mingle with us today ; promising not only to guard these mute memorials of their lives, but to cherish the memory of their heroism and loyalty, so that being dead they shall yet speak in the renewed devotion of thousands to our common country.

We sincerely thank you for this beautiful hall, consecrated as it is by the memories of the dead, which you have so kindly committed to our care and use. We assure you that the privilege shall never be abused, and that this hall shall ever be a rallying point for the soldiers of Berlin. And when one by one they shall have passed to that better land, we trust their names may be added to these, and that loyal and true men will then be found to honor and cherish the names of all.

POEM, BY MR. JOSIAH BRIDE.

For years I've ranged through circles far away,
And know so little what you do or say
In Berlin, and so seldom I appear
Among you, that I scarcely have a sphere
Of action with you. Importuned to write,
I yield ; and I should do so with delight
If I could feel that I possessed the power
To create scenery for this favored hour.
With small inventive powers and no wit,
I cannot shine or sparkle here one bit ;
And I must write, as everybody knows,
In verse such as I have, or feeble prose.
Yet I am asked to take the poet's lyre,
Without the poet's wit or poet's fire.
How dare I here presume to touch the string,
Lest harsh and jarring notes discordant ring?
High, high presumption it may seem in me,
And yet I see,—at least I think I see,—
That, with much confidence, I may depend
Upon your kind indulgence to the end.
What such indulgence is I full well know ;
I have been favored with it long ago ;

And few, if any, can have higher claim
To love this people, love the very name,
Berlin, (that thrills the soul when far away,)
Than he who speaks to you in verse to-day.

When, far from home, they ask me where I live,
And I'm disposed correct reply to give,
I say, " in Massachusetts," and am proud
To have it heralded in any crowd.
And when they ask me in which county I
Reside, I haste to make them this reply :
" In Worcester county," far more truly great
Than any other county in the State.
Then, if they more minutely question me,
And ask me in which town I love to be,
" Berlin," I say, " by me is loved'the best,
And more to be desired than all the rest."
And, though my inmost soul delights to soar
And range the distant universes o'er,
I soon return, and, when my wings are furled,
I find the centre of my social world.
I love the people of this town the more,
Because I knew them in the days of yore :
And I was educated, *grew up here* :
And, though imperfectly I filled my sphere,
Bending the twig, training the opening mind,
I found kind sympathies that few men find.
The heart's fond aspirations outward flow,
Both to the present and the long ago.
The present flits before the admiring eye ;
Deep graven on the soul the by-gones lie :
The nows may be more beautiful, more bright,
The thens may be as dear, as useful quite.
Man seems almost triune, but one, yet three—
The past, the present, and the yet-to-be.
We cannot well dissect this threefold man,
It may be that the doctors present can.
Should we divide with them, and choose our part,
We would prefer the region of the heart :
The heart we'd carry with us as we cast
A loving look upon the distant past.

When thought leads back to near the fortieth year
From this the present one, the one now here,
It shows us three physicians, strange to say,

Who, while they practiced here, found time to pray
To God—to render Him the highest praise,
And to acknowledge Him in all their ways.
All three stand with us on life's fleeting shore:
May blessings rest upon them evermore.
Prior to this 'tis said a Brigham stood
In this profession; was a doctor good,
Peace to his ashes and to all the race:
Justice assigns them no unworthy place.

In Doctor Brigham's day we had
   Not half as many people;
One little store, just one, no more,
   A church without a steeple.

No town-house neat, in which to meet,
   Discuss each public measure,
And there and then select the men
   To execute our pleasure.

In the house of God—however odd
   It seems—were held all meetings,
Where, without noise, the girls and boys
   Exchanged their social greetings.

And in the pews all talked of news,
   Profane and sacred matter,
Where, sitting down, the entire town
   Made a tremendous clatter.

In the altar stood our Puffer good,
   Though mercury was at zero,
And frozen nose, fingers and toes,
   Showed heroine and hero.

But the desire to have a fire
   Might then have raised a question
Whether the thought were not inbrought
   By Satan's vile suggestion.

But a Sabbath School, when not too cool,
   To the old church nobly stepped in,
And some noble souls, as on time rolls,
   Have up to this moment kept in.

All honor, all praise to the Puffers and Fays,
   And the Marys that stood around them,
To the tender love, earth's wisdom above,
   And richer than gold, that bound them.

Full forty years ago our Doctor Puffer
Went home; and can a grateful people suffer
His name to perish? No! all answer no:
And in the world to which such good men go,
Methinks the spirits flitting to and fro,
And all the holy angels, answer—no!
Men, such as Doctor Puffer, never die.
They live, may be, to thrill the hosts on high,
And in this world such influence may extend
Till sun and moon and time and being end.
Oft when the good man stood erect, upright,
Deep aspirations rose and took their flight
Till heaven seemed bending, till earth seemed to rise,
And all seemed floating in the upper skies.

In years quite young, and business matters old,
A citizen, about this time, struck gold.
Fountains were filled, from which rich streams are flowing,
How wide, how deep, we have no means of knowing;
But we are well assured, somehow or other,
They are kept open by a younger brother;
And though he should no deeper pierce the mountain,
He has for life a self-supporting fountain.

'Tis said by many, though denied by some,
That near this time there was a flood of rum.
Not deep as Noah's, o'er the tallest steeple,
But ruined fifty times as many people;
Swept off rich farms or ruined them forever,
Recovered by their former owners never.
We saw the flood—it rose not very high,
It did not wet, it made the people dry:
Some floated, some sunk deeper every day,
We saw them sink, but seldom heard them pray.
Upon that flood we never thought of shipping,
But promptly signed the pledge and left off sipping.

Soon after this subject, to wholesome rule,
Both sexes found with us a boarding school.
This school helped make a man that here we see,
And since that time he has been making me.
Well, that's all right—it's only tit for tat;
We don't complain of this, nor he of that.
But as he then seemed to enjoy our teaching,

So we, more recently, enjoy his preaching:
And in his higher school we now may see
Many a boy and girl once taught by me.
Josiah, Henry, Albert, Silas, Georgie,
Sarah, Sophia, Phebe, Mary, Morgie;
One was a very pleasant talking creature,
Smiling and laughing out through every feature.
How could we ever think to find another
So social in this world or any other.
He has her in his school, remains her Proctor,
Though she has long been boarding with the Doctor.
And Mary Grace, by record, now appears
To have been in his school twenty-five years;
He is so kind we have no cause to weep her.
His choicest treasure may he ever keep her;
Keep her to aid him in his deep desire
To lift each way-bound, struggling pilgrim higher;
Teach her and others until we are o'er
The river, on the bright Elysian shore,
Where rills of knowledge sparkling as they go,
From heaven's exhaustless fountains ever flow.

But of the future we will not now speak,
Our subjects in the past we'd rather seek;
Credit the bell-men for their matchless ringing,
Houghtons and Sawyers for their splendid singing—
Especially the latter, who the stages
Drove till the period seemed almost like ages,
And rode through spaces, in the speeding cars,
That might be thought almost to reach the stars,
Doing, for thirty years, all our expressing,
Being, in business matters, such a blessing;
If he could hear us, we would tell him how
We've missed him in this world, even till now.

South Berlin there was once a pleasant Park in,
Though there might not have been a single Larkin.
These birds flew westward, settled at their will,
Domesticated they remain there still.
Our Merriams have been honored without lack;
Fays, Sawyers, Fosgates, all have made their track;
And when our population was quite thin,
Carters and Wheelers rolled some big loads in.
To Joneses, Goddards, Bruces near our rills,
Barnes, Babcock, Spafford, Pollard on our hills,

Priest, Bigelow, Holt, Fry, or great or small,
We bring due honors—not to one, but all.
And last, although not least, we proffer now
All honor due the Elder Central Howe.
Thus here we memorize the souls departed
From every family, the noble hearted,
The spirits lifted to the upper spheres,
Crowned with the honors of the by-gone years.

Sadly we consecrate Memorial Hall
In honor of the brave men doomed to fall
Mid crash of arms and harsh, wild battle cry,
Or in the crowded hospital to die.
Imperishable as time be every name;
Let none despoil them of their dear bought fame;
But let the hand to infamy be wed,
That mars the laurels of the martyred dead.

Having thus wandered through the dear old past
With heartfelt gratitude, we now may cast
Our vision forward, and with faith may see
A far more dear, a brighter yet-to-be,
Honor the present as the ancient men,
For now true worth inheres in man as then;
Hence honor to our citizens, that they
Have built the house we dedicate to-day.
All honor to the brain that drew the plan,
All honor to the workmen, every man,
All honor to the man that gave the site,
All honor for *sweet harmony, all right.*
May heart to heart be bound with stronger ties,
Higher and higher may this people rise,
And mid diversity of mind God given,
No more may social bands be rudely riven.

In report of remarks by speakers from abroad, the committee of publication only claim to have given the ideas, in the main, without asking for written copies.

REMARKS OF MR. ARTEMAS BARNES.

Berlin was formerly the southeast corner of Lancaster, a corner of Marlborough on the southeast, and one farm taken

from Lancaster on the west. It took about one-third of the
town of Bolton. It does not appear to have a very early
history. It was considerably inhabited by the Aborigines,
and was probably passed over by soldiers in the early Indi-
an wars, and by the first settlers of Lancaster and Marlborough.

The first inhabitants were probably from the adjoining
towns of Lancaster and Marlborough. The name of Priest,
I should think, was one of the oldest, and also Moore, and
Maynard, and Wheeler, and probably Sawyer, still later.
And there were the Joneses and Goddards, and Carlisle in
the Marlborough section ; also three brothers Bailey, and
three brothers Johnson, who all had large farms adjoining
each other. One of them had one of the three largest
farms in Bolton. They were among the active ones in form-
ing and incorporating the town. These, with many others
that I might mention, were the original settlers of the town.
This southern and remote part of Bolton was called by
some, for the want of a more euphonious name, "Pussy,"
from the great quantity of that weed that grew in that part
of Bolton.

When the time had arrived that they were able to support and maintain christian worship, as was the custom and
rule of the Commonwealth at that time, they applied to the
General Court for an act of incorporation as a town, but it
was incorporated a district, with all the rights of a town,
except the right to choose a representative to the General
Court ; then they had to go to Bolton, which always caused
unpleasant feelings. In 1812, I think, the assessors found
there were the requisite number of ratable polls to entitle
them to become a town ; and Bolton voted that they might
separate. They then were incorporated a town, and have
continued to prosper and increase about as fast as other
agricultural towns in the vicinity. In 1800 there were be-
tween seven and eight hundred inhabitants in the town, and
in 1860 over eleven hundred.

The chair suggested that one of the Selectmen occupied
the place long occupied by his father, and represented honorably an honorable ancestry, original settlers of the town.

L. L. CARTER responded that in his opinion Berlin had blown its horn pretty well for that day, but he would say that having opposed the building a new town-house till the majority acting with him became the minority, he then took hold with the majority in good earnest, and was in favor of a good building that should do honor to the town, and he should now work as zealously as any one to help pay for it.

In response to the remark that a young man, having completed his education, thought his native town too small for his professional talents, and therefore settled in the large town of Northborough, leaving this little field for the chairman, DR. J. J. JOHNSON said:

What does the town-house express ? The elevation of the people. The secularization of religion. Once the higher themes of life were discussed by the few ; now by the many. The town hall and the lyceum are the common arena. When the few dominated in the opinions of mankind, bigotry was rampant and persecution triumphant. The reading room, the library and the town hall have taken the masses out the control of theological disputants, and of all who would rule by dogmatism. Recurring to Berlin as his early home, though not his native town, he recalled many pleasant associations with the families then resident here—some of whom especially he was glad to meet on so pleasant an occasion.

REV. DR. ALLEN, of Northborough, being called upon, gave reminiscences of Rev. Dr. Puffer, first minister of Berlin.

Called to preach the election sermon, through the influence of Judge Brigham of Westborough, as was customary, Dr. Puffer wrote out his prayer in behalf of the legislative body. In the exercises he faltered painfully. A fellow senator nudged Judge Brigham, and whispered, "That is your minister, is it !" But the joke did not last. The preacher soon gave up what he had committed to memory, and trusted to the occasion. Few men were so devoutly impassioned in prayer, and recovering his self-possession.

he poured out his heart-felt desires in strains of moving supplication. At the close of the prayer, the Judge returned the nudge of his neighbor, saying, "That is my minister." This sermon gave the minister of Berlin such reputation that the Faculty of Harvard College invited him to preach the Dudlean Lecture of that institution. In this he was equally successful, and the students and government of the college subscribed so liberally for the discourse to be printed, that the minister obtained a handsome remuneration. He afterwards received the doctorate from the college. Dr. Puffer was minister of Berlin from 1781 to 1829.

The chair remarked that if Dr. Johnson was not a native of Berlin, a man who was a genuine native, who had retired from a successful business in Boston to a neighboring town, would respond for the natives of Berlin, and also for our Mother Bolton.

S. H. Howe, Esq., of Bolton, said he was never ashamed of his native town, nor would he countenance any approbious epithet applied to her. He despised the man who would not recognize the place of his nativity because obscure, so that when traveling with a friend whose home was in an obscure town, but who registered his name as from Worcester, he on the contrary wrote his name connected with Berlin, the latter in letters so large they could be read three miles off; and that his goods were marked Berlin, and could have been found all over the land. When he settled in Bolton, he always registered from that town.

To the sentiment. "Worcester—a thief on the young men of Berlin," Amory A. Bartlett replied:

He acknowledged his connection with the county jail, but not as a thief. He had a Sabbath school class in that institution. When he went there and reported himself as being of Berlin, the superintendent replied, "We don't know Berlin in this institution." But Mr. B. was sorry to find in his class a lad who once had lived in our village. The boy began here by stealing fruit. Mr. Bartlett admonished the youth to beware of the first offense against honesty and uprightness.

"Foreign teachers of our Berlin schools ; we appreciate their services, but are not so well pleased when they make reprisals on our young ladies."

S. I. RICE, of Northborough, was called upon to answer. He recalled former experiences in Berlin, and saw before him some fruit of his labors among the town fathers on the platform. He remembered, too, his obligations to Berlin, not alone in the matter suggested by the sentiment, but he recalled the old town-house which this had cast in the shade. There they heard lectures and held lyceum discussions, in which he indulged in some of his early efforts at debate. Mr. Rice commended the appropriateness of the new edifice as becoming to the town.

The School Committee having been called upon, MR. E. C. SHATTUCK, on their behalf, said :

MR. CHAIRMAN,—I wish to make a little explanation. You said in your address that the project of a town-house on your plan, and the building committee also, were subjected to ridicule by some of the citizens, or words to that effect. Now I suppose you meant me ; at least the coat fits, and I put it on. I do not remember that I indulged in any ridicule at your expense as chairman of that committee, but I trust you will pardon me if I did silently harbor some doubts as to your ability to accomplish a work so much out of your line of business, to the general satisfaction. Though knowing that you were gifted in your profession, it did not occur to me that your genius was universal. I admitted, with thousands of others, that you could, out of products of nature, manufacture the "Key to Health" better than any one else ; but I did not know that you could, from the same source, gather the material and erect a town-house that would meet the general approval, and silence all criticism, for the very low sum stipulated.

But such appears to be the fact. I hear but one sentiment, that of praise ; and I am happy to say that whatever may have been my feelings at the work in the prospective, I am gratified with the work completed.

I would be glad to say something to the soldiers on this

occasion, but the lateness of the hour forbids any extended remarks. I yield to no one in my respect and esteem for those brave, patriotic men, who went at their country's call and nobly and unflinchingly did their duty. May they live long and be worthily remembered.

I wish to say a word to my fellow-townsmen. Gentlemen, you are soon to meet in this hall for the first time in your sovereign capacity, to transact important business. I trust that all will deport themselves in a manner becoming the place and the occasion. Let no one defile this beautiful floor with the juice of *that weed!* Let no one be so ambitious to rise in his position as to stand upon these clean settees with his boots on. Let no one mar any portion of them with pencil or jackknife. In short, let no one commit any act here that he would not wish to have daguerreotyped and handed down to posterity.

REMARKS OF MR. P. B. SOUTHWICK.

MR. CHAIRMAN.—I would say, in the language of Daniel Webster, in his address on the 17th of June, after the completion of Bunker Hill Monument. "A duty has been performed." For many years the town of Berlin has required a more suitable building for a town hall. On my return to my native town, after an absence of thirteen years, I felt more strongly than ever the necessity of a new building, and at all the meetings where the subject has been brought before the town. I have strongly urged the necessity of immediate action ; and although for a while with the minority, public sentiment changed so that I found myself with the majority, and the result has been the house in which we are now assembled—a building, though not very expensive, yet good enough for Berlin, corresponding better with the general surroundings of the town than a very expensive one would have done. And the committee who planned and built the same deserve much credit for the moderate expense incurred. And when the business and growth of the town demands a larger hall. I trust the citizens will dispose of the present and build one suitable for the occasion. But for twenty years to come the house is large and expensive enough, and one of which we may well be proud when compared with the old one.

After the remark that Clinton was a thriving, successful town, and had great and prosperous enterprises, but nothing more thrifty or satisfactory to the people of Berlin than her *Courant*, Mr. W. E. PARKHURST, its editor, replied very appropriately, in commendation of the town and its new town-house.

GEO. A. COTTING, Esq., of Hudson, replying to the remark that a native of Berlin who had long lived near us and shown his interest in us, and assisted in promoting "Justice and Peace" in the county, it was hoped had not lost, by removing to another county, his commission, at least to speak, said :

He had always been interested in Berlin, and all that pertained to it ; and in discharge of his duties as U. S. Marshal, he was proud to hail from Berlin, and make the returns of other towns from her office, and the name of Berlin would be found on all those returns at Washington.

"Our neighbor just over the line, who still instructs his native town in the principles of agriculture"

WARREN E. MOORE, of Northborough, responded, acknowledging the interest he still felt in Berlin as his native town. At present he would appeal to parents, and mothers especially, to remember that in training the youth of the town they were setting scions in the stock of the tree. Society would become what the rising generation should make it.

RECORD OF BERLIN SOLDIERS

LIVING AT DATE.

The Adjutant General's Report on the Infantry Service in the war has not been published as yet. The following record is therefore unavoidably incomplete. Our Town Clerk has copied to a large extent from the State documents. The committee have also been aided very much by Mr. ANSEL SNOW, whose situation as hospital clerk gave him extensive acquaintance among our soldiers in service.

It is proposed by the Encampment John B. Gough, Post 54 of the Grand Army of the Republic, in this place, to keep a record of such particulars of Berlin soldiers as may yet come to light, and be of interest in future years. Families and friends of soldiers are requested to communicate.

BERLIN SOLDIERS ENLISTED FOR THREE YEARS.

EDWARD BARNARD, son of Edward and Margaret, born in Boston. Enlisted June, 1861, Co. F, 13th Regt. Discharged by surgeon's certificate, February, 1863.

SAMUEL E. FULLER, son of Samuel M. and Catherine, born in Sunderland. Enlisted July, 1861, Co. F, 13th Regt. Discharged by expiration of term of service.

JAMES B. FULLER, son of Samuel M. and Catherine, born in Berlin. Enlisted as musician. Discharged with the band.

AUGUSTUS HARPER, son of James and Judith, born in Roxbury. Enlisted July, 1861, Co. F, 13th Regt. Discharged by surgeon's certificate, February, 1863.

GEORGE F. MASON, born in North Dana. Enlisted July, 1861, Co. F, 13th Regt. Discharged from naval service, August, 1863, by order No. 72, of Rear Admiral Porter.

JONATHAN P. MANN, son of Andrew and Lydia, born in Upton. Enlisted July, 1861, Co. F, 13th Regt.

SEWELL H. MERRILL, son of John D. and Mary H., born in Hampden, Me. Enlisted July, 1861, Co. F, 13th Regt. Discharged by surgeon's certificate, February, 1863.

ELLIOT A. RICH, son of James and Sally, born in Northborough. Enlisted July, 1861, Co. F, 13th Regt. Discharged by surgeon's certificate, January, 1863.

EDWIN H. RICH, son of James and Sally, born in Northborough. Enlisted June, 1861, Co. F, 13th Regt. Wounded at second battle of Bull Run, in the leg; at Gettysburg, in the wrist. Discharged by expiration of term of service.

CHARLES H. ROUNDY. Enlisted July, 1861, Co. F, 13th Regt. Discharged by expiration of term of service.

FRANCIS B. RUSSELL, son of Samuel, born in Wayland. Enlisted July, 1861, Co. F, 13th Regt. Discharged January, 1862, for deafness.

JOSEPH M. SAWTELL, son of Ebenezer and Roxanna, born in Berlin. Enlisted July, 1861, Co. F, 13th Regt. Promoted to Sergeant. Discharged by expiration of term of service.

DAVID S. SAWYER, son of David and Lavinia, born in Leominster. Enlisted July, 1861, Co. I, 25th Regt. Discharged October, 1864, by expiration of term of service.

DANIEL B. SNOW, son of Ansel L. and Catherine L., born in Nantucket. Enlisted September, 1861, Co. I, 25th Regt. Discharged October, 1864, by expiration of term of service.

CHARLES H. SNOW, son of Charles and Lucy, born in Bilerica. Enlisted October, 1861, Co. I, 25th Regt. Discharged October, 1864, by expiration of term of service.

ELI SAWYER, Jr., musician, son of Eli and Azuba, born in Berlin. Enlisted October, 1861, Co. I, 25th Regt. Discharged October, 1864, by expiration of term of service.

DARLING S. WHEELER, born in Richmond, N. H. Enlisted September, 1861, Co. I, 25th Regt. Discharged October, 1864, by expiration of term of service.

SOLON WHEELER, son of Oliver P. and Harriet, born in Keene, N. H. Enlisted November, 1861, Co. I, 25th Regt. Re-enlisted December, 1863. Discharged by expiration of whole term of service.

JOHN Q. MAYNARD, son of Winsor and Cynthia, born in Marlborough. Enlisted August, 1861, Co. D, 22d Regt. Wounded in left foot at Fredericksburg. Discharged September, 1864, by expiration of term of service.

FREDERICK MILLER, son of Phillip and McLean, born in Baden, Germany. Enlisted September, 1861, Co. D, 22d Regt. Wounded in left arm, May, 1864, at Spottsylvania. Promoted to Fourth Sergeant. Discharged September, 1864, by expiration of term of service.

AUGUSTUS M. STAPLES, son of Joseph and Sarah, born in Oxford, Me. Enlisted August, 1861, Co. D, 22d Regt. Discharged September, 1864, by expiration of term of service.

HENRY MORAN. Enlisted August, 1861, 22d Regt. Re-enlisted in Connecticut cavalry, and served through the war.

DANIEL W. WARNER, son of John and Sarah. Enlisted August, 1861. Promoted Sergeant Discharged October, 1862, by surgeon's certificate.

THOMAS KIRBY, son of John and Ann, born in Nova Scotia. Enlisted October, 1861, Co. II, 26th Regt. Discharged by expiration of term of service.

JOSEPH STAPLES, son of David and Elizabeth, born in Portland, Me. Enlisted December, 1861, Co. II, 29th Regt. Discharged Februray, 1864, by surgeon's certificate.

GEORGE C. WHEELER, son of Levi and Olive, born in Berlin. Enlisted December, 1861, Co. II, 29th Regt. Discharged by expiration of term of service.

ISRAEL F. CARTER, son of Ivory and Olive, born in Berlin. Enlisted August, 1862, Co. I, 36th Regt. Wounded in right breast at battle of the Wilderness. Discharged June, 1865, by special order No. 22, series 1865.

HARVEY J. CHASE, son of Lorenzo and Judith, born in Haverhill, N. H. Enlisted in Co. I, 36th Regt., Aug. 6th, 1862. Discharged June, 1865, by expiration of term of service.

AMORY T. MAYNARD, son of Winsor and Cynthia, born in Bolton. Enlisted Aug. 6th, 1862, Co. I, 36th Regt. Promoted Third Sergeant, September, 1863. Discharged September, 1864, by reason of consolidation of the companies in new regiment.

ANSEL SNOW, son of Ansel L. and Dorcas L., born in Nantucket. Enlisted Aug. 6th, 1862, Co. I, 36th Regt. Promoted Corporal, August, 1862. Discharged June, 1865, by reason of special order No. 22, series 1865.

GEORGE F. FLETCHER, son of Ariel and Hannah, born in Boston. Enlisted Aug. 6th, 1862, Co. I, 36th Regt. Wounded in hand in a charge on the enemy's works at Petersburg, June 17th, 1864. Discharged June, 1865, by reason of special order No. 22, series 1865.

OSCAR W. HOLT, son of Warren E. and Miranda, born in Iowa City, Iowa. Enlisted August, 1862, Co. I, 36th Regt. Discharged June, 1862, by reason of special order No. 22, series 1865.

JOSEPH E. KIMBALL. Enlisted Aug. 6th, 1862, Co. I, 36th Regt.

NATHAN M. ALLEN, son of Nathan and Harriet, born in Pittsfield, Vt. Enlisted Aug. 13th, 1862, Co. I, 36th Regt. Transferred to V. R. C., July, 1864, Portsmouth Grove, R. I., and discharged September, 1865, by expiration of term of service.

JOHN F. CROSSMAN, son of John W. and Eveline, born in Bolton. Enlisted Aug. 6th, 1862, Co. I, 36th Regt. Discharged March, 1865, by special order No. 77, on surgeon's certificate.

JOHN F. MARTIN, son of Patrick and Mary, born in Utica, N. Y. Enlisted Aug. 6th, 1862, Co. I, 36th Regt. Discharged by expiration of term of service.

SPENCER C. CHAMBERLAIN, son of Spencer C. and Lucinda T., born in Thetford, Vt. Enlisted Aug. 6th, 1862, Co. I, 36th Regt. Discharged May, 1865, by reason of special order No. 22, series 1865.

OLIVER SAWYER, son of Ira and Abagail, born in Berlin. Enlisted as musician, Aug. 6th, 1862, Co. I, 36th Regt. Discharged June, 1865, by reason of special order No. 22, series 1865.

44

WILLIAM H. KING, son of Nathaniel H. and Mary E., born in Lynn. Enlisted Aug. 6th, 1862, Co. I, 36th Regt. Discharged June, 1865, by reason of special order No. 22, series 1865.

WILLIAM H. HORTON, son of David and Melinda, born in Dorchester. Enlisted Aug. 6th, 1862, Co. I, 36th Regt. Discharged by special order No. 22, series 1865.

CHARLES A. HOWE, born in Leominster. Enlisted June, 1862, Co. F, 13th Regt. Discharged by surgeon's certificate, February, 1863.

WILLIAM B. CAMPBELL, born in Lovell, Ct. Enlisted in Co. B, 11th Regt., June, 1861. Discharged by expiration of term of service.

LEVI H. HOLDER, son of Daniel and Harriet, born in Berlin. Enlisted in 27th Regt. Left the regiment in mental aberation.

AUSTIN GILL, born in Worcester, son of Peter and Bridget. Enlisted July, 1861, Co. F, 13th Regt. Wounded in foot at battle of Petersburg. Discharged at expiration of term of service.

JOHN ROBBINS, born in Stow. Enlisted June, 1861, Co. M, 3d Cavalry. Discharged 1865, by surgeon's certificate, at Dale Hospital, Worcester.

OLIVER P. WHEELER, son of Joseph and Betsey, born in Swansey, N. H. Enlisted June, 1864, Co. B, 3d Cavalry. Injured in spine by fall of horse in battle. Discharged November, 1865, by surgeon's certificate.

GEORGE E. MAYNARD, son of George W. and Sophia, born in Berlin. Enlisted June, 1864, Co. B, 3d Cavalry. Discharged by expiration of term of service.

CHARLES F. STAPLES, son of Joseph and Sarah, born in Portland, Me. Enlisted December, 1863, Mass. Heavy Artillery. Discharged September, 1865, by expiration of term of service.

JOSEPH C. BADGER. Enlisted December, 1863, Mass. Heavy Artillery. Discharged September, 1865, by expiration of term of service.

JOSEPH W. MERRILL, son of John D. and Mary H. Enlisted December, 1863, Mass. Heavy Artillery. Discharged September, 1865, by expiration of term of service.

JAMES F. RATHBURN, son of Solomon and Hannah, born in Berlin. Enlisted December, 1863, Mass. Heavy Artillery. Discharged September, 1865, by expiration of term of service.

SAMUEL H. HAYNES, son of Emory and Anna, born in Wayland. Enlisted December, 1863, Co. B, 59th Regt. Wounded in side at Poplar Grove, Sept. 30th, 1864; same day in left leg, which was amputated below the knee. Discharged July, 1864, at Dale Hospital, Worcester.

WILLIAM WILSON. Enlisted in 5th Mass. Cavalry, November, 1864.

CHARLES M. LOVEJOY. Enlisted October, 1864, 1st Regt. Mass. Vols.

MARVIN DAY, Jr. Enlisted October, 1864, in 4th Mass. Battery.

GEORGE MUNROE. Enlisted November, 1864, in 2d Mass. Infantry.

HENRY GREY. Enlisted November, 1864, in 1st Mass. Cavalry.

AUSTIN KIRBY, son of John and Ann, born in Worcester. Enlisted April, 1862, in 5th Heavy Artillery. Discharged September, 1865, by expiration of term of service.

DAVID R. BROWN. Enlisted 1861, in Vol. Reserve Corps.

PHILO BRUCE, son of Sewell and Eunice, born in Berlin. Enlisted September, 1864, for one year in Mass. Heavy Artillery. Discharged May, 1865, by special order of War Department.

JOHN A. RILEY. Enlisted in Navy, 1861. Discharged, 1865, by expiration of service.

ENLISTED FOR NINE MONTHS' SERVICE.

FRANCIS BABCOCK, son of Ephraim and Mary, born in Berlin. Enlisted September, 1862, Co. I, 5th Regt. Discharged July, 1863, by expiration of term of service.

HARRISON T. BABCOCK, son of Josiah and Betsey, born in Berlin. Enlisted September, 1862, Co. I, 5th Regt. Discharged July, 1863, by expiration of term of service.

WILLIAM T. BABCOCK, 2d son of Albert and Mary, born in Berlin. Enlisted September, 1862, Co. I, 5th Regt. Discharged July, 1863, by expiration of term of service.

CHARLES H. BLISS, son of Henry H. and Maria, born in Berlin. Enlisted September, 1862, Co. I, 5th Regt. Discharged July, 1863, by expiration of term of service.

JAMES M. BULLARD, son of Joel and Judith, born in Berlin. Enlisted September, 1862, Co. I, 5th Regt. Discharged July, 1863, by expiration of term of service.

WILLARD G. BRUCE, musician, son of Sylvanus and Hannah, born in Berlin. Enlisted September, 1862, Co. I, 5th Regt. Discharged July, 1863, by expiration of term of service.

GEORGE ELLIS, son of Philo and Charlotte, born in Berlin. Enlisted September, 1862, Co. I, 5th Regt. Discharged July, 1863, by expiration of term of service.

HENRY R. HOLDER, musician, son of John and Caroline, born in Berlin. Enlisted September, 1862, Co. I, 5th Regt. Discharged July, 1863, by expiration of term of service.

AUGUSTUS L. HASTINGS, son of Reuben, Jr., and Caroline, born in Lancaster. Enlisted September, 1862, Co. I, 5th Regt. Discharged July, 1863, by expiration of term of service.

GEORGE W. HOWE, son of Isaac and Rebecca, born in Leominster. Enlisted September, 1862, Co. I, 5th Regt. Discharged July, 1863, by expiration of term of service.

LEWIS T. HOWE, son of Emphraim, Jr., and Susan, born in Berlin. Enlisted September, 1862, Co. I, 5th Regt. Discharged July, 1863, by expiration of term of service.

FRANKLIN W. PAGE, son of Jacob and Mahitabel, born in South Boston. Enlisted September, 1862, Co. I, 5th Regt. Discharged July, 1863, by expiration of term of service.

JOHN A. MERRILL, son of John D. and Mary H., born in Frankfort, Me. Enlisted September, 1862, Co. I, 5th Regt. Discharged July, 1863, by expiration of term of service.

RUFUS C. SAWYER, son of Rufus and Seraph, born in Berlin. Enlisted September, 1862, Co. I, 5th Regt. Discharged July, 1863, by expiration of term of service.

DAVID B. WHITCOMB, son of Eleph and Harriet, born in New Ipswich, N. H. Enlisted September, 1862, Co. I, 5th Regt. Discharged July, 1863, by expiration of term of service.

ENLISTED FOR ONE HUNDRED DAYS.

WILLIAM T. BABCOCK, 2d son of Albert and Mary, born in Berlin. Enlisted July, 1864, Co. I, 5th Regt. Discharged November, 1864, by expiration of term of service.

CHARLES A. BARTLETT, son of Amory A. and Jane, born in Berlin. Enlisted July, 1864, Co. I, 5th Regt. Discharged November, 1864, by expiration of term of service.

JOSIAH W. BRIDE, son of Amos and Hannah, born in Berlin. Enlisted July, 1864, Co. I, 5th Regt. Discharged November, 1864, by expiration of term of service.

WILLARD G. BRUCE, son of Sylvanus and Hannah, born in Berlin. Enlisted July, 1864, Co. I, 5th Regt. Discharged November, 1864, by expiration of term of service.

EDWARD H. HARTSHORN, son of Edward and Elizabeth, born in Berlin. Enlisted July, 1864, Co. I, 5th Regt. Discharged November, 1864, by expiration of term of service.

AUGUSTUS L. HASTINGS, son of Reuben, Jr., and Caroline, born in Lancaster. Enlisted July, 1864, Co. I, 5th Regt. Discharged November, 1864, by expiration of term of service.

GEORGE L. HOWE, son of Lyman and Rebecca, born in Marlborough. Enlisted July, 1864, Co. I, 5th Regt. Discharged November, 1864, by expiration of term of service.

WILLIAM H. TENNEY. Enlisted July, 1864, Co. I, 5th Regt. Discharged November, 1864, by expiration of term of service.

DAVID B. WHITCOMB, son of Eleph and Harriet, born in New Ipswich, N. H. Enlisted July, 1864, Co. I, 5th Regt. Discharged November, 1864, by expiration of term of service.

HENRY E. BROWN, son of Ira and Amelia H., born in Berlin. Enlisted July, 1864, Co. I, 5th Regt. Discharged November, 1864, by expiration of term of service.

FRANK E. BROWN, son of Ira and Amelia H., born in Berlin. Enlisted July, 1864, Co. I, 5th Regt. Discharged November, 1864, by exyiration of term of service.

BENJAMIN F. WHITTEMORE, born in Virginia. Enlisted as chaplain July, 1862, in 53d Regt., for nine months. Discharged by expiration of term of service. Re-enlisted as chaplain in 30th Regt. Mass. Vols., for three years.

www.ingramcontent.com/pod-product-compliance
Lightning Source LLC
Chambersburg PA
CBHW032121080426
42733CB00008B/1009